Father Browne
at
Home

A personal memoir
by J. C. Martin

Father Browne at Home

First published in 2009 by Swiftmartin Publishers Limited

First edition, First Impression

Copyright © of this material has been asserted by the author and publisher

Copyright © by Swiftmartin Publishers Limited
The Mill
Tinahely
Co Wicklow
Ireland

ISBN 978-0-9562097-0-2

Reproduction by Altaimage, London

Cover: Fr Browne photograph by RJ Martin, mirror image.
     "Village" photograph by Fr Browne, "After Gold Hill"

Printed and bound in Great Britain by Butler Tanner & Dennis, Frome, Somerset

Father Francis M. Browne 1880-1960

I dedicate this book to the fond memory of uncle Frank and those like him who brighten
our lives with their photographs.

Photographs from 1894 to 1937 – Volume I

Contents

Next year, 2010 marks the 50th anniversary of Father Francis Browne's death. Its advent provides the impetus for a revue of Frank's story that illustrates his singular perception of the twentieth century. It is likely that further volumes will be required to cover his account in pictorial record. It has been a winding path to follow the milestones of his career as priest and photographer set against the background of the two world wars but I hope to construct this book from Frank's point of view to present a reflective afterlight as he may have wished.

This work was performed by assembling the threads of his personal experiences as illustrated in the family photographic archives and more cogently by the personal descriptions of his life where the darkest hours were recorded by his niece in her first world war diary, and his finest by his nephew, Robert Joseph Martin, consultant Ear, Nose and Throat surgeon, Frank's friend and lifelong companion.

This volume may no doubt show some shortcomings. Taken altogether they nevertheless suggest an account of events in Frank's life as he may have interpreted them, sometimes in ironic contrast to the historical events that occasionally surfaced during his career; the worse the news the better the picture! For Frank who had seen so much joy and sorrow there was the odd bitter rosary. But it may be discerned that he had determined to create his pictures as a testament to the peace and understanding he sought in his career leavened with the multi-coloured textures of humanity so gleefully combined in his photographs.

One may imagine it easy to present an image of how he was, at ease, at home, with his infectious humour and bubbling conversation, where his ideas tripped over one another in cascades of anecdotes and aphorisms; all conjoined with a measured interpretation of events and insightful comments on the human condition. But many of Frank's photographic compositions are so telling they require no further information, unless he gives it on the reverse. It may be useful while turning these pages to recollect events at the time the pictures were taken, to catch a glimpse of the layers behind this renaissance man's mind and how he distilled the information before him into the creation of his next photograph.

Preface

Acknowledgements

The compilation of this picture book has been greatly assisted by the vivid memories of Frank himself and all the uncles and aunties who were very aged when I was small, and who slipped away too soon; but who left so many memories in their diaries, letters and notes regarding Frank's life. Most of all, to my grandfather Mr R.J. Martin: for his help, patience and generosity in the family affairs and for leaving me his photographic records since his birth in 1898.

More recently to my mother Ursula, who identified many of the obscure characters on film and what they said and did. For her permission to include some family photographs that outline her development and continuity through Frank's lens.

To those who encouraged the formation of the book, Gabriel Haughton, Father E O'Donnell and Stephen Baty who reconnected me with the craic. To Mathew Kellet, Reece Newton and Paul Jackson who's expertise enabled this book to come to fruition. To Rob King at Altaimage whose production of these images as historical documents have captured the nuances in Frank's printing process. To Edward Byrne for identifying some of Frank's locations and to Colin Rynne. To Liz Moore who kick started the process and to Paul Camp and Peter Howell who pointed the way to publication.

Above all, to my dear wife Sarah, who has patiently overseen my wellbeing in the long hours when ideas and information were coming together in between rearing our children and keeping us in good order.

"Behind the cover"

Father Browne at Home. . . An Introduction

Up till the latter part of the twentieth century, the photographic genius of Frank Browne, who became an Irish Jesuit priest, was only known to his close family. He and his nephew, R. J. Martin, had spent much of their leisure time taking photographs and spending many subsequent hours in their darkroom, as well as relaxing at home with R.J's family. For Frank, it was a passion that started in the late nineteenth century and continued up until the middle of the twentieth. R.J started at fourteen years of age in 1912. Besides Uncle Frank's well publicised pictures of Ireland, his Great War experiences, and his short trip on the ill fated Titanic; he also recorded English life and that of his family. Frank Browne's images weren't fussy, he liked what he saw and captured it with his camera; but he had the knack of being able to take pictures that look good. Frank's greatest legacy is a memorial to all those like him who were camera fanatics, but whose pictures were lost.

Although Father Frank Browne was destined to play an important role in the history of photography, relatively little is known about the man himself. My grandfather was R. J. Martin, and I had the privilege of working beside the two of them in the family darkroom in Cheshire, England. Frank was a constant visitor to our house, and as a boy, sitting round the fireside with the family one evening, I asked him where we came from and he replied with a chuckle, that we might have come from an ancient line of Irish horse thieves! He may have been near the truth because many of his photographs make the history, life - and horses of the west

coast fascinating to anyone with an interest in them. His interest in the myths incorporating the known Celtic, Viking and medieval antecedents had been with him since he was a boy, so it is no surprise to find, as recent research suggests, that tribes of the Western Isles contain an offset trace of DNA unique among the shifting populations of Europe. The Brownes follow a tortuous lineage back to the famous tribes of Galway; as do the Joyces. Frank knew James Joyce from his school days and Joyce mentioned him in his writing.

Frank was the youngest of nine children, of which only one brother James and one sister, Margaret, went on to marry and bring up a family. Frank's mother died just after his birth and he became very attached to Margaret and her subsequent family and spent his time with them when not in the company of his religious colleagues. It was there in the cradle of new life that Frank experienced the notion of a family at work and play, and where photographs of himself and new members of his family survive.

Soon after Frank became of age in 1900, his life was punctuated by a series of events so extreme as to be unimaginable to most mere mortals; his lucky escape from the Titanic and his chaplaincy to the Irish Guards in the First World War, where he miraculously escaped death, though not injury, as hundreds of thousands of others were slaughtered before his eyes. His eldest brother, James, a doctor in London, always managed to find him when he returned injured from the trenches making sure he

was expertly patched up. But besides the horror of that war, also on his mind were the fellow passengers of the Titanic who had drowned in the icy waters of the Atlantic. He carried the memories of those horrors for the rest of his life.

Because of the close relationship between him and his elder sister Margaret, he became a close friend of his nephew, my grandfather, her only boy, who also became a doctor; this bond was to last to the end of their lives. With their mutual love of photography, they produced thousands of photographs together, which remain in the family archives. The photographs in this book illustrate the first phase of Frank's invaluable record of the period and show the progress of his 'wider' family through the travails of the twentieth century until 1937.

These photographs record and reinforce Frank's principal attribute as a perceptive observer and they illustrate, through his faith and photography, his view on the innate perfection of creation and the importance of family life to hold that creation together. As his work as priest and photographer grew in importance, he accumulated a reputation for a clarity of vision and an easy open-mindedness. He combined these with a traditional view of paths to salvation that culminated in his popular role as master of ceremonies to missions and retreats throughout Britain and Ireland. On the secular front, he was involved in setting up the Camera Club of Ireland, which is still active today.

A recent chance discovery brought to light the diary of Frank's first niece Philippa. Her reflections, particularly those on the Great War, brought to life an age when a whole generation was sent to their deaths and where she says of her Uncle Frank "Thank God for a real friend". The diary informs us of Frank's many visits on the way to and from Ireland and lead to the first compilation of Frank Browne's photographs at home. While a few are missing, the ones that survive delineate a pictorial record of Frank's unusual life and interests, together with some favourite photographic compositions that suggest a deeper meaning to his work. One may suspect that many of his photos shared a common programme; the aim of which was to express a well defined message. His personal representations of people and places are paced in this book by his regular return to his brother's and sister's families.

Frank's triumph is here depicted in his vision of humanity. Wherever he went, he recorded the fruits of peoples' work, and here shares with us their progress. Frank's deep philosophical and religious beliefs are graphically combined with this vision to form some of the finest examples of his pioneering snapshot style.

Chapter 1

Early Life

"Teach us good Lord

To serve thee as thou deservest;

To give, and not to count the cost;

To fight and not to heed the wounds;

To toil, and not to seek for rest.

To labour, and not to ask for any reward;

Save that of knowing that we do thy will."

St Ignatius Loyola, founder of the Jesuits 1550
  - Extract from the Queen's speech, Christmas 2007
  - Reading at the Cenotaph, Nov 2008

There are Brownes with an 'e' in England, Ireland, Germany and Scandinavia. Francis Mary Hegarty Browne born in 1880, youngest son of the family of the Mayor of Cork in Eire, was the last in his line.

One of Frank's first family photographs shows Ellen Browne, the Bishop's sister, affectionately known as Auntie Cobh, with Hilda and Janie – James Browne's children, circa 1894.

The Browne, Hegarty and Booth families in the Bishop's garden

Frank's mother died within hours of his birth and various aunts helped look after the children. Frank stayed with one of them in Dublin while he attended day school, with James Joyce, at Belvedere College. After she died in 1893 he went to Castlenock College as a boarder.

Lafayette

30, WESTMORELAND ST
DUBLIN.

It was his uncle, made Bishop of Cloyne in 1894, who kindled his lifelong love of photography by giving him an Eastman Kodak No1 and then sending him and his brother William on a visit to Europe. There are few pictures of this European tour, but some postcard shots of Florence and Venice show an appreciation of composition. Though the brothers may not have had time to absorb all they had seen first time round, it is apparent that Frank had been much affected by the lucidity of the Renaissance artists; Leonardo, Raphael and Tintoretto's religious, mythical and historical subjects are a few whose moments are brought to life in Frank's later work. Their essays in chiaroscuro would shade his view of the major events of the next century. In the meantime, Frank had decided to train as a Jesuit priest, and during his novitiate often had his camera confiscated. Where he hid his cache of film is not recorded. . .

The Bishop's House and HQ

The Bishops new project, the spire to St Colman's Cathedral.

1894

Uncle William and the new Kodak Brownie with Mr Kelly and the cousins.

Killiney Strand.

1900

Three momentous events occurred in 1898: Firstly, his nearest and dearest sister Margaret gave birth to her only son, Robert Joseph in England, attended by Frank's eldest brother, Doctor James Browne: who had also emigrated. Secondly, came the tragic news that their father had died while taking his daily swim at Crosshaven. Brother James was in Ireland for a holiday and had the onerous task of signing the death certificate. Thirdly, his second brother was reported missing in South Africa after the Zulu wars. Twenty years later, Frank looked for his grave.

Notwithstanding, the following year Frank went up to the Royal University of Ireland, from where he graduated with a BA Hons in Classics. This is where he may have learned to mix his metaphors for which he was renowned. One of his contemporaries there was James Joyce, also a former pupil of Belvedere College, also from Cork and sharing an interest in photography.

At the turn of the century, while Eire's economy had barely recovered from the Famine, the urban drift of uprooted labourers meant that Dublin, like other European towns and cities, was growing fast. Up to half the domestic dwellings were ranked as tenements and similar to new industrial developments in other countries, many of those were barely shelters thrown up by the rural, but hopeful dispossessed. The trials of the holy family in the stable spring to mind, but he would have been aware of the hardships and choices those people had to make. Great issues were at hand: Gladstone and Parnell were negotiating the fundamental human rights of the Irish in the Home Rule Bill; meanwhile Parnell's mistress was divorcing her husband, causing public indignation to the Catholic majority. In South Africa, Irish soldiers were now fighting alongside the British Army in the Boer War and Queen Victoria visited Eire in recognition of their contribution.

"The Holy Family" drawn by Frank's eldest sister on the occasion of Bertie Martin's birthday. The artist, Sr. Mary Josephine, became a nun and latterly PR to Pope Pious X.

Bertie Martin was born 1898

Frank's elder sister Margaret Browne, born 1872 and the only sister to marry, with her husband Jerome Martin, surgeon and physician of Cork who qualified at King & Queen's College Of Physicians in Dublin 12th October 1883.

Queenstown quays.

The British Navy hang out their washing at Hawlbowlin. 1908

'Horses on the Poop Deck' – Frank took three trips to Italy before 1904.

The Pope's summer palace at Gandulfi, north of Rome.

Glass plate exposure.

But Frank was to travel back to Italy again, where he joined the Jesuit fraternity of the most highly developed theological minds in Europe and embraced a life of religious contemplation and meditation. This would culminate in a series of compound exams in cosmology, epistemology, ethics, logic, theodicy and psychology. These were to be deliberated verbally as a hundred theses in disputarium with the most eminent philosophers of his time; with his peers in attendance, in Latin. This fearsome regime took place at the Jesuit community in Turin, however, during the summer breaks the novices were free to travel, staying at Jesuit houses on the way.

One wonders how Frank could have reconciled such a keen artistic sense as he had with the discipline of his calling – until these informative three years come to mind. It must have seemed like heaven to a young Irish novice; a trip to Venice is unforgettable and in Florence, in the Uffizi alone, galleries full of Renaissance masterpieces are breathtaking. Indeed the ethic for the whole of Michelangelo's work was to 'move the soul inexorably towards God', and the photographic clarity of Caravaggio's religious paintings show visions of ecstasy with details considered, assembled and perfected in the many dimensions of human existence that enveloped Frank in this city where the Medici's had once ruled! Together with his one hundred theses, Frank wrestled with those mighty ghosts of the Renaissance as if his life were a succession of stark and irrevocable choices, with salvation and damnation perpetually at stake.

A glance through his old textbook on Platonic cosmology belies a thorough grounding in Sophocles' sense of fun, and Frank's wicked sense of humour no doubt reflected his years of study in Jesuit institutions. As with most educational establishments concerned with concentrated religious enlightenment for months on end, the development of a hobby helps to pass the time and Frank was happy to record it.

On his return from Italy, as the next stage in Frank's progress to becoming a priest, he returned to one of his old schools, Belvedere, as a teacher. There he founded the Camera Club, which is still going today. If he needed any excuse to photograph everything around him, this was it. His pictures reveal a sense of wonder at the people's progress and show trains, boats and planes. There are several of crowded beaches, which indicate that the populace had increased leisure time. On the other hand, some of his pictures show open sewers running down the street – although the people are smiling.

His first number one hit, so to speak, resulted in 1904 he travelled with his brother Will by sea to Rome, where his sister Mary was part of the papal household. Through her, Frank met the visionary Pope Pious X (who swiftly acquired sainthood), whom Frank photographed. It is hard to underestimate the impact this photograph had on the Catholic world. The soft-framed portrayal of a man radiating infinite goodness, widely believed to echo God's word on earth, was printed by the hundreds of thousands.

The next few pictures selected from Frank's early photographs illustrate local scenes that fired his interest, some with his two young nephews; Bertie and Clifford at the Bishop's house. He must have gone exploring with them to Blarney Castle and rivers on the way. On one of his trips they discovered a plane leaving for America - although he did not go himself!

These photos were taken between 1904 and 1910

May St Pius X
watch over & protect
Bertie, Etta, W.J. and Children
and may
the Blessing he gave to Uncle Willie
+ myself & to all our dear ones
in April 1904
be with you ever

After we had been at his Private Mass
we,
Uncle Willie & I,
Chose this as the best likeness of him
that we could find in Rome

With love from Uncle Frank
June 16th 1954

Frank may have sent the postcard slightly late –
fifty years later! . . by this time Pope Pius X
had become a Saint

"The Lady Passenger"

The first transatlantic flights took off from Shannon, being nearest. This may have been a trial run. . .

The Hon. Lady Antoinette, James Browne's wife, is with a friend, and her son Clifford is with his cousins, Bertie – jumping- and Phillipa Martin, sitting on the grass. Frank, their uncle, took the picture circa 1909. Bishops House.

Blarney Castle, the two nephews.

"River Boys"   1909

"Clapper Bridge" with Frank's shadow

Frank tried several shots of this local beauty spot
Then as now there can be complications with the old silver
nitrate negatives. The girl is collecting
berries in a basket.

"Walk the Plank" – The inimitable light on the west coast

"A great tribute to the Bishop"

One airy tale suggests that this shot inspired Walter's fairy tale castle in Disneyland.

26

The tender 'America' awaits the Titanic.

"Moonshine"

"The optical telegraph receiver"

Titanic. Anchors aweigh.   1912

Local Irish lace makers were allowed on board to tempt the passengers.

"Dogs on Deck" – There were three dogs on the Titanic, including Robert W. Daniels' champion bulldog just purchased in Britain.

Chapter 2
Titanic

In 1911 Frank left Belvedere and began another period of study, leading to his ordination. The following year, at the age of thirty two, he passed his hundred theses by viva voce with flying colours. Imagine the excitement when he received the ticket, via his Uncle, inviting him onto the maiden voyage of the Titanic ~ the talk of Eire and the wonder of the world. Frank's ticket was for a voyage to his destiny, but the destination was only to Cork via Cherbourg. To a penniless novice the occasion must have been equivalent of a trip to the moon!

Naturally he took his camera with him photographing every aspect of the journey: from Waterloo station in London where he caught the Boat Train to Southampton; the voyage itself; the ship and many of the passengers. On the voyage came a further invitation due to the largesse of a new acquaintance on board to continue the passage to America. However Frank had picked up a bug, or so he thought, and he was carried off the liner at Hawlbowlin' on a stretcher. This did not delay the Bishop, Robert Browne and his retinue from setting off on the pilot's launch from the quay at Queenstown to inspect the great ship, and after a pleasant afternoon they returned carrying Frank; full of tales about who they had met and seen on this grand occasion.

Frank took several more pictures of the ship as she slowly turned out of the majestic harbour. She was low in the water with her passenger list now swelled with Irish emigrants on their way to the New World. He must have been feeling a bit shaky as he took the last picture, because he was diagnosed with a grumbling appendix which was to come back to him later. Notwithstanding, he set about developing and printing his treasures and, after labelling them, put them in an album which he presented to his Uncle. No one could have guessed the news of that great ship's destruction. Most of the faces that gazed out from the pages would never be seen again. Frank's album contains the only comprehensive photographic record of the interior of the Titanic, but at the time it had a practical use. Frank's photographs were printed on the front pages of the world's press and were directly

responsible for reuniting several lost families, including two French children who's father had eloped with their nanny, and perished with most of the passengers and crew. Their mother saw Frank's photograph from which she was able to identify them.

After a decent interval and some encouragement from the Bishop, Frank took on a series of illustrated lectures about his experiences. He was fascinated by the new wireless technology of Marconi. Frank took the only photograph of the Marconi room on board.

Frank also took many pictures of the Titanic's sister ship, the Olympic, which funnel band identifies the ship above.

Of the photographs Frank considered for his Titanic album there were some he omitted because of minor discrepancies: too light, too dark, out of focus, duplication. These last few that did not make the album still illustrate Frank's mastery of his craft.

Signals!

The Bishop's entourage approach the Titanic.

September 9th 1912

Later that year some clues to everyone's whereabouts came to light in a stray postcard. Frank was on holiday in England from the seminary at Miltown Park and incidentally stopped to partake in one of the popular Aeroplane Circuit Races. At the same time, his nephew and niece are on a touring holiday, staying with a Mrs Turner in Hathersage, Derbyshire, where they recieve his latest postcard. The village has a number of stone circles in the vicinity and is close to the picturesque Peak District. The card is perhaps obscure: addressed to them both as "Master Philippa B. Martin". It is possible at the age of fourteen that Bertie and Philippa are on a field trip before returning to school.

Frank suggests they "Don't forget Wingfield. . .it requires reading beforehand to reconstruct the history of the place". Now a spectacular ruin, Wingfield was a subject of interest to Frank as the last home to Mary Queen of Scots, once a cause celebre with the Jesuits, but not so by Queen Elizabeth the 1st!

Frank further enquires if they have a copy of "Set in Silver", a charming vignette by a lively Victorian lady who describes her favourite journeys around England with some pleasant pictures. Frank recommends they visit Fr Bursche, the local Jesuit priest. Only then does he mention that "the flying race here yesterday was a failure owing to big wind. Bertie mind you get good photos for me. I want them for slides. D.O.F".

Bertie, addressed as "B" on the card, and his sister produced some stunning snaps, including this one of High Tor, opposite. Frank may have used his time off to join them because a complete album shows their efforts were satisfactory, with prints of different shades that suggest a developing student on the Leitz enlarger.

"DAILY MAIL" AEROPLANE CIRCUIT, 1912.
H. SALMET, WITH HIS 50 H.P. BLERIOT MONOPLANE. HOLDER OF BRITISH RECORD FOR HEIGHT, 9,000 FT.
LONDON TO PARIS SPEED RECORD, 3 HRS. 12 MINS., AND OVERSEAS DISTANCE RECORD, EASTBOURNE
TO DIEPPE, 80 MILES.

Philippa had taken the train to Bakewell with "Aunty" Cobh, the Bishop's sister, with whom holidays were exchanged in Queenstown on a regular basis.
"Soon after we left the direct road to Hathersage and turned to the right up by the moors – to think of Elizabethan days & the fugitive priests hiding on those desolate moors. . ."

It seems that Frank's advice was well founded because –
"We were walking down a steep hill when suddenly without warning a large grey mass set in the midst of yellow fields sprang into sight. Wingfield!

As I walked down the lane I thought of Wingfield's siege – Newcastle and his men pressing forward to help the defenders. Strange I could not make Mary of Scotland live though I tried – we explored some of the building before tea – we saw the crypt and several more rooms. Before leaving Stuart Faire & I raced up to Queen Mary's tower and down again."

Frank's niece and nephew, Philippa and Robert, had spent several summer holidays in the peak district and these were described in Philippa's diary recording their progress. She describes the setting for the photograph: "The afternoon sun was shining. Everything was bright. The water held cool green deeps & shallows & I gazed & dreamed. . ."

"High Tor" – written on the reverse side

Clongowes Wood College *Centenary of June 1st 1914*

Frank had a fine physique and was a good rugby player at school. His interest is reflected in snaps of his pupils at Belvedere and of his nephew Robert in long forgotten matches. Robert was at school at Clongowes Wood College in County Kildare; having heard that his nephew was attending a very good, though Protestant, school in England, Bishop Robert had arranged for his namesake to have, as far as he was concerned, a more suitable Catholic education in Ireland.

CLONGOWES Wood College, Kildare, Ireland.

Bertie Martin waits at the entrance gate. May 1914. He is sixteen years of age.

Frank appears in a 1908 tall Edwardian De Dion Bouton motor car with an unidentified female companion in black.

"Irish Bishop, Father Kane, Uncle Robert."

Father Nolan Sj keeps an eye on Frank. Father Kane is bending the Bishop's ear.

Father Nolan, right, observes Uncle Robert standing left, in conversation with John Redmond MP.

"John Redmond signing autographs"

An aerial view of Clongowes – taken with an ingenious contraption with Frank's Kodak hanging from a kite!

Each photograph in this series describes the time, date, place and exposure on the reverse with an added caption. This habit was to stand Frank in good stead throughout his life as preacher, teacher, conciliator and raconteur because it could be discerned in his conversation that he could elevate most situations to tally with one or more of his fifty odd thousand captions and never be stuck for a topic upon which to expand!

Frank's inquisitive nature was rewarded by the sense of occasion at the Clongowes Wood College Centenary of June 1st 1914; which presents a comprehensive collection of luminaries with his uncle, the Bishop and local MP, John Redmond in the top hat.

June 3rd 1914: a match in progress in front of the old pavilion

"C.W.C Match against the "Crescent of Limerick" – 1915

Many of these boys playing in a muddy field in Eire ended their lives in another muddy field on the Somme.

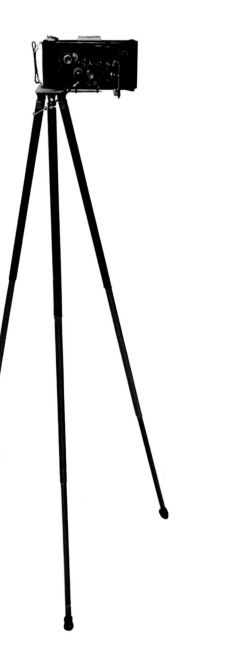

Father Frank Browne Collection *No 11 & 15*

Frank used the Eastman Kodak the Bishop had given him for twenty five years until he got the Plaubel Makina in 1919, see page 57.
The Kodak is unusual in that its German lens is a Carl Zeiss Jena Tessar f10.5

Frank, Will and the Bishop.

In 1915, Frank was solemnly ordained into the priesthood by his uncle in his cathedral; St Colman's in Cobh. This wonderful edifice was one of the last pure High Gothic cathedrals ever built in the French style, which from a distance, displays quite fairytale proportions. All the experts had been consulted in the building and finishing off the details. The influence of the architects Burgess and Pugin abound under Ruskin's critical eye; whose philosophy had extended to the furthest quarters. Bishop Robert added the tallest spire that would fit, making it the last landmark many passengers saw on the voyages west.

Chapter 3

The Great War

As if in slow motion, the world stumbled towards the greatest confrontation in history, and the new Father Browne was put forward as chaplain to the Irish Guards in care of officers, men and thousands of country boys; many of whom he had taught at school. A uniform – and shoes – some grub everyday, a jaunt to Gay Paree and back before Christmas? It was too good to be true.

Frank looked pretty grand wearing his new uniform sitting on his horse, as this postcard to R.J shows –

Frank's brother William signed up to join the convoys. His nephew R.J, just nineteen years old, had been drafted into the army and was at training camp at Berkhamsted in Hertfordshire, bound for the trenches.

Raw recruits - little did they know.

Father Browne, The New Chaplain to the Irish Guards

"Fix bayonets! Present Arms!"

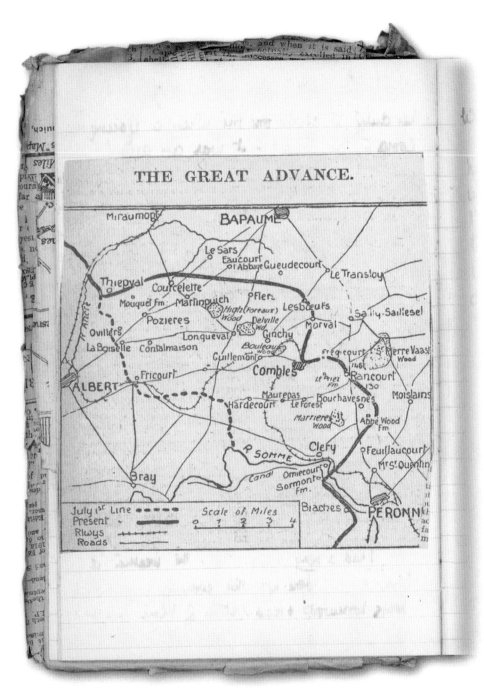

THE GREAT ADVANCE.

Father Browne's few pictures of the Great War lean towards a celebration of life against fearful odds. We know at least one of his peers survived; the indomitable Father Scanlon, who became a fine example of the priesthood and Frank's confidant after the war. Frank often brought him home to visit us. The two priests had witnessed horror beyond words, but Frank always tried to steer the tone of his conversations towards levity. He never mentioned the war. Of the few amusing incidents, my grandfather told me – "When he heard the shell coming over he pushed the King off his horse into the hedge - and got a medal for it!"

However, what details filtered through were described in his niece's diary and a few extracts hint at the mood: 1916 "Monday Sept 11 – Read in the paper the news of the great Irish advance at Guillemont – also of O'Dwyer V.C.'s death. Sometimes as now – the heartrending sorrow of war grips one & tears one to pieces. The first hundred thousand I am reading also leaves a lump in one's throat"; the number refers to the men killed in the first battles of the Somme.

Philippa illustrated her thoughts with maps of the advancing lines and newspaper cuttings of our troops' progress together with cut out strips of obituary notices posting the death of her many young male aquaintances – "Thurs. Sept 21. I heard yesterday of Franklin Willmers death. He was such a sportsman. So clever & good & sporting & handsome. I remember six years ago when he as Captain of the School was leaving how he thrilled us with admiration of the big splendid fellow – and now he is dead. Today I heard of George Dinan's death. R.I.P. – The deaths last week were awful awful.
We're winning but all the best men are going – its too harrowing for words – the shadow of war is on me & I cannot be content.

Sat Sept. 30 – We heard the other day that Uncle Frank had been wounded – we know no details"

Irish Guards - off to war

Another Rock Ferry Officer Falls.

was a good fellow in everything. Always enthusiastic, he never failed doing the right thing or saying the necessary word. He loved Birkenhead School, and in return his "Alma Mater" at Shrewsbury-road fos-

Lieut. R. D. PATERSON.

tered and produced the highest qualities of a nature which was charged with the great instincts and inspirations of his class. His end is regrettable, but the manner of his death is linked up with the best traditions of our race.

Poor Paterson! R.I.P.

He was so handsome & had such a lovely voice. I haven't seen him for years but remember when he used to be a great 'swut' at B'head School where I admired him so much long long ago.

"Fri. Oct. 20 – heard that UF is in London undergoing an operation"

The diary reflects a microcosm of how the war affected life at home, and Philippa had spent much of October 1916 preparing for the next tea dance – all her friends were involved but:-

"Wed. Oct.25 – the dance must be put off owing to falling off of men. Alas! - so depressed.
Then – Uncle Frank arrived tonight – Sat. Oct.28.

Sun. Oct.29. Went to Uncle Frank's Mass – spent most of the day listening to him.

Thurs. Nov.23 – Courage! I'm walking deliberately with a swagger in order to force myself into my usual outlook on life – I dressed for the University dance. It was such a nice dance. Bertie was a darling in getting me partners and I danced with two men who won the Military Cross. One of them Capt. Deane was an awful flirt.!

Thur. Dec.7 – Met Malcolm Glover home wounded from the Somme – poor kid he said it was hell –
P.M. Asquith's eldest son killed."

About 3.30 a telegram was handed to me from Uncle Frank. It said 'Meet me 8.30 tonight usual place. Frank'

I got a shock. I knew he was to send the telegram but I never thought he'd do that - Of course he & Aunty thought that an extravagant telegram would be great fun never dreaming that Miss Smith would open it - but she did & 'phoned in haste to Mother to practically tell her that her daughter was planning an elopement. Mother howled with laughter.

I went home early & had a good old talk with Uncle Frank. Thank God for a real friend.

We went to see Fr Van den Haute who is certainly the most tactless man I've ever met. Fancy on an occasion like that asking me why I didn't go to daily Mass & appealing to Uncle Frank

I was simply furious & could barely keep my temper but I managed politely or fairly politely to shut him up! That's not the way to make me go to daily Mass. Of course I want to go (though I rarely get there) but his interference makes it doubly hard for me - and he's not my confessor either.

Uncle Frank told me I look much younger than I am & probably Fr Van den Haute doesn't know I'm as old as I am.

I did some revision while Uncle Frank & Mother went to the pictures & then had another long talk with him later. Fri. Dec 15. I stayed at home fairly late today to see Uncle Frank off. When I got to school I found them all quietly working away at revision. I joined them - Oh! I explained about the telegram to Miss Smith & she was awfully amused & quite nice.

Philippa's Principal at the teaching school was Miss Smith.

Frank's lovely photograph of his niece, Philippa and an unknown, beau was taken on top of Thursaston (Thor's stone) hill at the beginning of the war. The details and verse in a strange hand on the reverse are clear but the friend is a mystery.

'Their First Tiff'

on Thursaston Common
April 11th 1916.

Exposure.
1/25 sec F.9 Bright Sunshine
12·25 P.M. on Kodak N.C. Film
Printed on Vigorous Glossy Velox

Turn not thine eyes away,
Place your hand in mine,
Tell me sweet one just to stay
and let our hearts entwine

It was always assumed that the photo was one of Bertie and his sister – but he was just sixteen at the time and she eighteen. The verse is seductive; more redolent of Oscar Wilde or Yeats: but who was he?

Years later, Philippa's niece Ursula Martin was also here, with an Afghan hound.

Father Browne went over the top each evening to commend the souls of his men to their maker. His usual invocation was "I absolve thee in the name of... may you rest in peace. Amen." He was shot by snipers and wounded five times.

There was some space for the living. Rudyard Kipling, the writer and poet, arrived to mourn his only son. Father Frank rose in the pulpit amidst the live shrapnel of a shell shocked church, to exhort the buffs – "Are you more afraid of God or the Germans?" The great dark painting now at London headquarters, only shows a man on his knees blessing the shades of a thousand men before they too were shot.

It could be said that Father Browne demonstrated the professional handicap of a working priest for whom the complexity of the mystery can obscure the humanity of the men in his care, to look for a pattern where none existed. Father Browne emerged as the nonpareil of priesthood and he did understand the problem. But he knew that to understand is to despair. Kipling summed it up succinctly: "If any man asked why they died, tell them that their fathers lied."

Frank's commander and life long friend, Colonel (later Lord) Alexander, called Frank 'the bravest man I ever met', and ever tried to stop him going over the top armed with nothing other than his faith and his courage. Frank, winner of the Military Cross, the Croix de Guerre and the Belgian equivalent, left no cleverly edited version of himself. His uncensored letters home give little indication of his circumstances. Only a lone soldier in his photographic masterpiece, 'The watch on the Rhine' defines his singular predicament. The ethical concept reconciles Frank's last impression of the war in the best way he knew. The soldier symbolizes the end of the conflict. He is the only survivor, required to guard the crossroads of a conquered country. Although this picture invited the notion of closure, it seems to reinforce his intention to snap moments in time with a hopeful outlook on the future; but he constantly questioned it. Could he have been warped by the hypocrisy of the age? Could he reconcile a lost decent Ireland or achieve it only in the imagination?

On the ground, the practical aspect was fortuitous; he had, after witnessing years of industrial suicide, got a new camera and some plates, and was itching to use

them for a peaceful purpose in a conquered land. But how to become the 'happy snapper' in times like these, with his jaw still wired up, his wounds stiff and that mustard gas still rattling in his lungs? Frank's battalion entered Germany victorious and took up headquarters in Cologne, at the foot of the mighty, dark Teutonic Cathedral of St Ursula, so different from his uncle's airy creation at home. In 'The watch on the Rhine' the twin spires of the Cathedral point high behind the soldier. A quarter of a century later the spires were the only thing left standing when Cologne was obliterated by the Allied bombers. And half a century after that the author took part in a stone conservation project there.

The new camera helped provide consolation for Frank's pasting on the battlefield. As a spoil of war, the Plaubel Makina was a German press photographer's camera that required loading in the dark with rather unwieldy glass plates. However it was the large Carl Zeiss Jena 2.9, 1-10cm lens that caught his eye. The war momentarily forgotten, Frank set about learning the intricacies of his new toy and after a hesitant start took several pictures with it. His new interest was shared with his brother William in a series of letters that give no hint of past pain. Together with his other things, the Makina is working today with some spare plates. Some have not yet been developed.

In 1919, at the age of thirty nine, Frank resigned his commission and quit the killing fields. On his way back to Ireland he stopped in England to visit his nephew, Robert Joseph Martin. Bertie had joined the army as a stripling, but had been taken out of the ranks when it was discerned that he was qualified to train as a doctor, like his father. He attended Liverpool University where undergraduates were 'pushed' through the system because of a shortage at the front. Frank's racking cough suggested a trip to warmer climes but when he arrived at the Bishop's house he found parts of Cork were burning, courtesy of the Black n' Tans. The next we heard of Frank was pedalling his bicycle up to the English lines to plead for the life of one of his old pupils who was involved; he was hung at dawn anyway.

Frank shared with many ordinary people the feeling that they didn't know where they stood any more. Frank felt their confusion and loss. What more could he say to the mothers and children in the streets where no men returned at all?

Brixham Barge Race

Father Browne's health continued to be of concern and finally his superiors decided to send him on a trip to Australia to recover. Upon his return Frank and R.J followed the trail of "Set In Silver." On their way back through England they paused to take photographs of picturesque villages, including the rural scene on the front cover of this book, with atmospheric shots of boats along the south coast.

Brixham inner harbour

Brixham outer harbour

"Home from home" Torquay harbour

Torquay Yacht Club

Prior to Frank's departure for Australia, Bertie had qualified as a doctor, and to Frank, was now elevated to R.J. He was moving towards his speciality of ear, nose and throat surgery. One wonders why he chose such a narrow field, but he remarked years later that as we had descended from a line of Catholic bishops and priests. . . it was better not to proceed below the collar!

Armed with his new qualification and an invitation from the Bishop, R.J and Frank arrived at the Bishop's house for an enjoyable holiday in spring 1921 -

But it became clear that Frank's symptoms were growing worse and it was here that a decision was made to send him abroad so that his respiration could recover. Frank wound his way around the world on a passenger ship, stopping off in South Africa, where he looked for the grave of his elder brother, Robert, and visited other countries en route. On the way back, in Ceylon, he posed with an elephant where he looks frail. While the hot, dry climate restored his lungs and well being, he was able to take pictures in Australia as good as the gold rush in America.

Meanwhile, R.J had married Etta, the matron at the Royal Stanley Hospital in Liverpool where they had been nursing thousands of W.W.1 casualties back to health. After a decent interval their only child Ursula was born in March 1926. For Frank, this was a major event because R.J's mother, Margaret was the only female in his immediate family to marry and her life outside the church was of the minutest interest to those who remained in it – one sister was a nun, one brother, William, parish priest of Blarney, and their uncle was the Bishop.

On his return to Europe, he presented R.J with some Boer bayonets as mementos of his trip. Though Frank's much diminished cough was signed off by his newly qualified nephew, he was gaunt after the war, his lugubrious face with a new twist to his noble chin where the bullet had passed through. His eyes were still steady, with a twinkle atop an aquiline Roman nose, set in a long face – a feature he shares with his immediate family; not so good with a bow tie, but excellent with a collar! Frank was given a clean bill of health and returned to Dublin to resume his duties.

BISHOP'S HOUSE,
QUEENSTOWN.

16 March 1921

My dear Bertie

Ten thousand Congratulations.
You have done magnificently.
All of us are rejoiced and
proud of you. B^r Martin
aged 22 !!! Long & happily
May you live to wear your
honours and by perseverance
in steady work to advance
from stage to stage to a high
place in your profession.
You will now try to become
a Resident for 6 months at
least in a hospital — but
the most pressing immediate
duty is to take a good rest
+ a healthful enjoyable

holiday. Would you come here
for a fortnight
Yours fondly
Uncle Robert

Dr Robert W Martin
Birkenhead

The photograph in the Bishop's garden shows R.J, Will, Ursula in the arms of Ellen, the Bishop's sister and secretary, and the Bishop, seated.

The date must be 1928, because Ursula looks at least two years old.
This snap could not have been taken by Frank because he would never have lost the Bishops feet!

Chapter 5 Between The Wars

On the Bog Road Achill

The Western Isles off the Irish coast produced arguably the best pictures of Frank's photographic career. Their desolate remoteness offered some spiritual detachment.

"That's how it works RJ & UF" – With every year that passed until the end of Frank's life, they met and set out to find the light.

One of the most beguiling aspects of Aran and the west coast is the predominance of ancient ruins, dwellings, churches, monastic remains, standing stones and curious massy monuments spread over a time range of several thousand years. There are some monumental pre-Christian fortresses that bring to mind the Berber casbahs in the high Atlas. This in County Mayo. Several structures on Aran perch on outcrops of limestone, and this may explain the multitude

of buildings there. Lime is used to bind the stones together, seal and finish the walls of traditional buildings. The great cathedrals and churches of Europe could not have been built without it. Throughout his life Frank sought out this metaphor of binding people and places together and no more so than in his pictures of this period which capture the timeless monumentality of his subjects in the hope of teasing out the mystery of their makers.

This spartan "Hermitage" belies a grand supply of fish under the bed.

Frank would have been delighted to find this exquisitely carved lancet arch standing in splendid isolation on the west coast. Arches have been known to give the spirit a lift to the beholder.

Typical of the early English or Gothic style, the Cistercian arch is common throughout Europe for its elegant simplicity. Frank photographed many Cistercian ruins while recording the subtle variations in the stone mouldings - including the dog-tooth or star moulding shown in several variations here within the intrados.

Frank photographed thousands of interesting structures and sketched several unusual buildings on the reverse of his prints.

"The Irony of it"

By this time he was working up to a thousand photographs a year and he wanted to join the dots of his disparate diversions. Besides, Frank had discovered

KEEL VILLAGE ACHILL

Achill Island, where he composed some of his best photographs, and here is one of his favourite subjects in black traditional costume.

He photographed many holy sites including this view, of Croagh Patrick, his first pilgrimage in 1926.

Frank had taken possession of a perspective equalizer so that tall buildings did not become distorted at the top of his pictures - although there are still a few fingerprints at the base of the tower!

From a professional point-of-view the accidental exposure to light below the base meant that this photograph was rejected. However the historical aspect made it important enough to keep in the archive.

Cloyne Tower, County Cork. Circa 1924.

Reflections –   *Father Browne's resourcefulness, innovation and daring, began to be recognized by his superiors and they accepted that his life could be reconciled as artist and priest. He demonstrated that the artist, whether in photography or anything else, was compatible with being a good priest. He heard confessions every Saturday, and his patient explanation and absolution were sought throughout the parishes.*

Kylemore Abbey –   *He regularly held masses throughout Ireland; his sermons were celebrated for their gimlet rhetoric. He took missions, attended committees and was much in demand to lead pilgrimages and celebrate retreats. He took time off for his photographic projects because many of these duties were held in the evenings, and also to visit us at home in England at least once a year.*

Frank enjoyed holidays in England as well, between taking missions at cathedral cities and convents. Of the many photographs of him there were more of his nephew R.J.

Frank's photo of R.J holding the new Zeiss Contax I was labelled "The Prevailing Passion." He soon exchanged it for the Contax II, because it was a lot easier to operate. Llanbedrog beach in North Wales was the setting for summer holidays. It shares some characteristics with the Kerry coast.

A picnic at Rhiadir falls, below, was an opportunity for R.J to show off his new car with the benefit of the new camera. One may almost hear him asking his wife to 'shake a leg' for the final snap which he sent to the Austin magazine.

Frank was very pleased at Bertie's photographic success, and as his mentor, I'm sure he would have wished to include this one.

JULY 1930

4 D.

VOL. 3
NO. 10

BEVERLEY NICHOLS on "The Woman Motorist"

The Austin

MAGAZINE

AND ADVOCATE

A JOURNAL OF ROAD TRAVEL

The old Plaubel Makina plate camera is still working.

Glengarif 1930

Aunt Mary, Frank's eldest sister, Auntie Cobh, the Bishop's sister and Uncle Frank looking solemn.

There was some sad news from England in 1931: Frank's niece Philippa had died. She had never married, and it is possible that the Great War had affected her at least as much as it had Frank himself. Her diaries record that her first fiancé and then every man in her close society was killed, missing or wounded in Flanders fields; their photographs, from the local newspapers, are glued on the pages. She reports that the popular tea dances were eventually attended only by women, before they ceased altogether. She writes of her great concern when Frank was reported to have been shot, and her relief at his recovery is palpable. Her account of the practical jokes he played at home are benevolent. Philippa, always delicate and elegant, became a good teacher and died when only thirty six years old, some say of a broken heart. Her written record of family life with Fr. Browne around, is the only one that survives.

But there was a great niece, Ursula, born to R.J and Etta in 1926. Throughout her development into a beautiful woman, Frank and R.J took hundreds of photographs that capture the innocence and joy that radiated through every aspect of her life at home.

Now a grandmother, Margaret played with Ursula in the family garden at Oxton, Wirral, with Peter, the Welsh terrier.

Frank's sister, Margaret Martin with Mac, the spaniel on Bidston Hill

Ursula by the stream

Ursula with friend in Achill

Etta and Margaret, R.J's wife and Frank's sister, at Poles Convent

Margaret, Etta and Ursula, Grandmother, mother and daughter, at Upton Convent c.1930

Meanwhile Frank was developing a complex relationship with the new Contax. He often said its lens somehow captured the soul of its subjects – particularly if the same lens was also used in the enlarger when printing. The realisation seemed to lift Frank's oeuvre to rare levels of clarity and his distinctive 3D pictures were finding their way into salons and exhibitions all over Ireland, a feat all the more remarkable because,

while Frank had studied the birth of photography, it was achieved without mimicking modern trends. Few examples of Frank's early work have been printed other than those he left at home. They are composed with a masterly touch, as if his subjects are progressing through time and space in answer to his question.

Achill Head.

Monumental vistas on this scale are a challenge because some panoramas are too big for the lens.

Time and space – Frank made them his speciality.

The logistics of a field trip without the family are illustrated in these 3 postcards fired off by Uncle Frank in the summer of 1937. In the first, Frank arranges to meet R.J in Dublin at the end of July. Again he asks if Uncle Willie can come. In the second, a week later, he writes to R.J's wife Etta enthusing on the "Great Photographic Work", by way of apology.

In the third he writes to Ursula on 9th August, saying the same thing but "I'm terribly sorry that I shall not see you this year". This was the first year that Frank had not seen his great niece. Frank's card to R.J with the cat is a rare example of 'out of focus' - because the cat moved! All this to enjoy a holiday by the sea.

ACHILL HEAD HOTEL.

View from Slievemore Mountain, Achill.

Achill landscapes . . .

Huisht! It's Fr Browne with the camera!

Bertie on the rocks.

At the end of day.

Keem Bay Achill.

1361

Frank augmented his resources by supplying the local hostelries with postcards!

Now you see him -

Here Father Frank swaps snaps with R.J, discussing the difference in angle points, composition, observation and perspective; of how too much light or shade can affect

the finish, white wall dazzle, particularly the highly reflective limewash, exposure, setting and framing - of yet another horse, portrayed outside the pub, of course.

Sláinte a la carte!

Achill Landscape

F.M.B. Sq.
1939